A

is for
ATTIRE

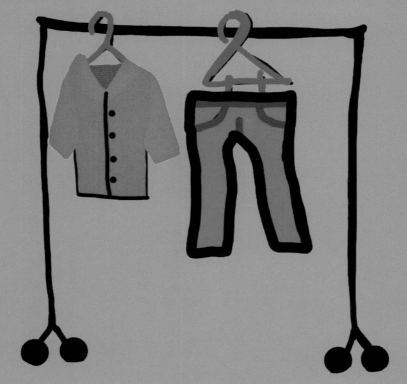

B is for
BOOTS

C is for CHIC

D is for DRESS

E

is for

EARRINGS

F
is for
FRAGRANCE

H is for HEELS

I

is for

I ♥ FASHION

J is for JACKET

K
is for
KIMONO

L

is for

LIPSTICK

M
is for
MINI
BAG

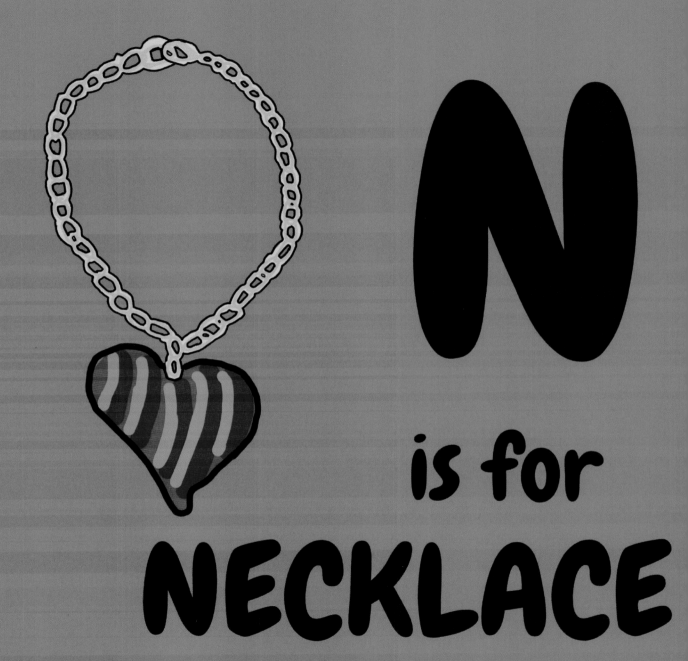

N
is for
NECKLACE

O is for
OVERALL

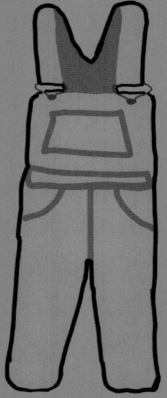

P

is for

PANTS

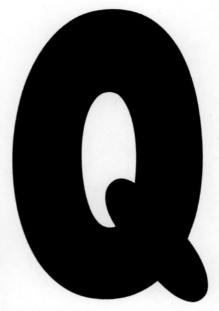

Q

is for

QUILTED CHANEL

R

is for

RING

S is for SWIMSUIT

T is for
T-SHIRT

U
is for
UNDERWEAR

W

is for

WALLET

X

is for

Y is for YARN

Z is for ZIPPER

Printed in Great Britain
by Amazon

24947196R00016